YOU AND YOUR BODY

Your Senses

Dorothy Baldwin and Claire Lister

The Bookwright Press
New York · 1984

YOU AND YOUR BODY

Your Heart and Lungs
Your Senses
The Structure of Your Body
Your Body Fuel
Your Brain and Nervous System
How You Grow and Change

Some words in these books are
printed in **bold**, and their meanings
are explained in the glossary on
page 30.

First published in the United States in 1984 by
The Bookwright Press, 387 Park Avenue South, New York, NY 10016

First published in 1983 by Wayland (Publishers) Limited
49 Lansdowne Place, Hove, East Sussex BN3 1HF, England.
© Copyright 1983 Wayland (Publishers) Limited.

ISBN 0-531-04798-9
Library of Congress Catalog Card Number 83-72788

Series designed by Behram Kapadia
Illustrated by Nicholas Cannan

Printed in Italy by G. Canale & C. S.p.A. Turin

Contents

Chapter 1

Your Senses

Imagine you have fallen off your bicycle. You are not badly hurt -- just a stinging knee. Forget the thoughts like "This bike is useless!" or "I know what I did wrong then." Think about how the information that you have fallen off your bike is collected by your senses.

SIGHT: This is easy. You can see yourself sitting on the ground, and your overturned bicycle.

It's easy to lose your balance like this if the grass is slippery.

TOUCH: Your knee is stinging, and you felt the jolt as you hit the ground.

TASTE: You won't taste much unless you bit your tongue when you hit the ground. Then you might notice the salty taste of blood.

SMELL: If you were going fast and tried to stop suddenly, you may smell burning rubber from your brakes.

HEARING: You can hear the noise as you crash to the ground, and the wheels of your bike still spinning round.

BALANCE: You may feel dizzy, a little shocked to find yourself on the ground — where you didn't expect to be.

Your sense organs

The parts of your body which collect information are called sense organs. They are your eyes, skin, tongue, nose, ears and inner ear. Notice that not just one but nearly all the sense organs pick up information at the same time. Can you work out which are the most important of your senses — and why?

All your sense organs have tiny nerve endings called **receptors**. They receive or collect information. They are very sensitive indeed. The information they pick up is called a **stimulus**. It travels quickly by electrical charge along the nerves to your brain. Only the brain itself can work out, or interpret, what each stimulus means.

How many senses can you see being used in this picture?

A stimulus flashes to your brain telling you the kettle is hot, and you pull your hand away.

What are your senses for?

Your brain is tucked up inside your skull — a long way from your finger and the steaming kettle. On its own, your brain wouldn't get any information from the outside world. The receptor nerve endings in your finger send the stimulus flashing up to the brain. In this way, sense organs do the important work of protecting you from harm. They also, of course, send information about the wonders of the world. Sense organs have sometimes been called the "gateways to the brain." Can you think why?

Stretch receptors

These are nerve endings which collect information about your "insides." For example: when your stomach is empty, your bladder is full, or your muscles are tired. They also keep the brain informed about where the parts of your body are. This is very useful as you don't have to watch your fork traveling up to your mouth, and you don't have to think where your smile muscles are before you smile. It takes babies some time to work out this information.

This baby hasn't yet learned exactly where his mouth is!

Chapter 2

Your Eyes and Sight

Many people think sight is the most important of the senses. Do you agree? Can you list at least ten things you couldn't do if you were blind?

How your eye is protected

Eyebrows stop rain and sweat from running into your eyes. You also use them to show strong feelings. Try looking angry or surprised without moving your eyebrows!

Your eyelids work as shutters, closing down to let your eyes rest. They also blink very quickly if anything dangerous suddenly comes too close. Most people blink about once every four seconds.

Your eyelashes work as traps, stopping bits of dust and dirt in the air from falling into your eye.

The **conjunctiva** is a transparent lining that covers your eyeball and the inside of your eyelids.

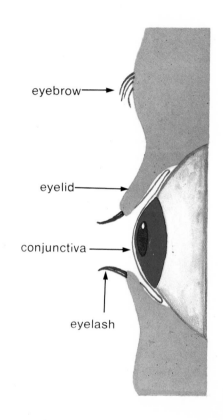

eyebrow

eyelid

conjunctiva

eyelash

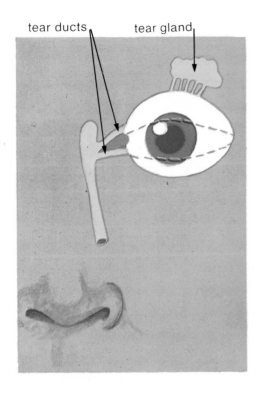

tear ducts   tear gland

In the diagram you can see where your tear glands are. They make tears — a clean, salty liquid — all the time. Blinking spreads the tear across your eye, keeping it clean and wet. The tear ducts at the inside corner drain the liquid into your nose.

When you cry, so much liquid pours out that the tiny ducts can't drain it all away. Teardrops form and run down your cheek. People can cry from happiness as well as sadness. Can you work out why you get a runny nose when you cry?

How light enters your eye

Study the two photographs carefully. One is taken in dim light, the other in bright light. The **pupil** is the hole in the middle. The **iris** is the outer colored part; it is made of rings of muscle.

Too much light will damage the eye, so the iris closes up, letting only a small amount of

Do you know which eye was photographed in bright light?

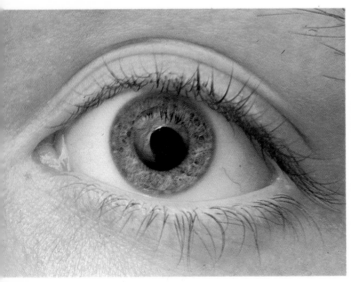

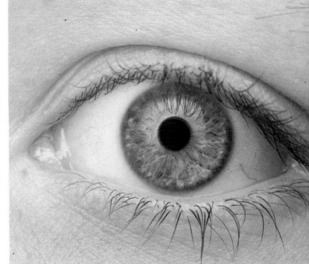

light in. When the light is poor, the iris opens wide to let in all the light there is.

Test this by sitting in a dark room with a torch in front of a mirror. Shine the torch into your face and you will see your iris starting to close.

Inside your eye

Behind each pupil is a **lens**. It is clear so that light can pass through. It is held in place by muscles and **ligaments**. Usually the lens is flat and thin when you look at something in the distance. But when you study, the muscles make your lens short and fat so that you can see objects close to you. The lens **refracts**, or bends, the light coming into your eye. A sharp image then lands on the **retina.**

The retina is a lining at the back of the eye made of nerve endings. These are light receptors. There are two sorts of light receptors: about six million **cones** which only work in bright light and pick up colors; and about 125 million **rods**. The rods work in dim light and cannot pick up colour, only the differences between light and shade. Light receptors are called rods or cones because of their shape.

The **optic nerve** at the back of your eye carries all the information picked up by the rods and cones to your brain. Like a camera, the picture of the outside world which lands on the retina is upside-down. The brain "turns it the right way up" as it interprets the messages from the retina.

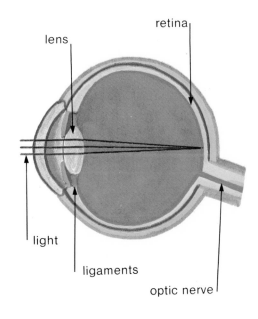

lens

retina

light

ligaments

optic nerve

Finding your blind spot

Where the optic nerve leaves the eyeball there are no rods or cones. This tiny area is your blind spot.

To find your blind spot, hold this page at arm's length and close your left eye. Look at the star and slowly bring the page towards you. When the dot vanishes you've found the blind spot in your right eye. Do this again with your right eye closed, and look at the dot this time.

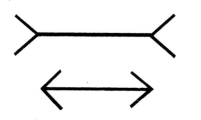

Are these lines the same length?

Is seeing always believing?

Well, what do you think? These diagrams are called **optical illusions**. Your brain is puzzled because the pictures don't seem to make sense. Optical illusions help to show you that it is your brain which interprets pictures — not your eyes.

Two faces or a white chalice?

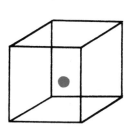

Is the dot at the front or the back of the cube?

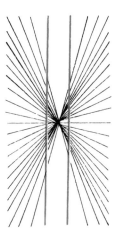

Are the red lines straight?

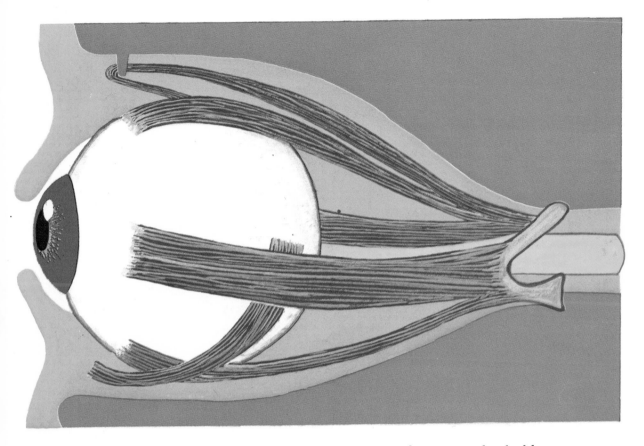

How your eyes move

Without moving your head, look up, then down, and from side to side as far as you can. Can you feel your eye muscles stretching? You have three pairs of eye muscles. They hold the eyeball in its socket and control your eye movements.

Ask a friend to look at his nose. That is one kind of squint. The three pairs of eye muscles should work together, but in new babies one eye may turn slightly inwards. As the baby gets older the squint corrects itself. If one eye stays "lazy," it must be treated by a doctor.

These muscles hold your eye in place and move it in all directions.

Using both eyes together is called **binocular vision**. Two eyes can see more than one and together they help you to judge distances. Point at something and close each eye in turn. Does your finger seem to move? This shows you that each eye sees a slightly different picture. Your brain interprets both of the pictures together.

It will seem to this boy that his finger moves from side to side as he closes each eye in turn.

Blindness and color blindness

Close your eyes and let a friend lead you about the room. Do you feel confused or frightened? Do you feel in danger? Blind people have to rely on their other senses to give them information about the outside world. This boy is learning to read through his sense of touch. His book is printed in **braille**, each letter being made of raised dots.

A color-blind person can usually see red and green, but cannot see shades of these colors. Scientists think this happens because of a fault in the cones. About eight percent of men are color-blind. It usually doesn't affect women, though color blindness is passed on from mother to son. Can you see the numbers on the test card? If you can't, tell your doctor and have a thorough eye test.

By using his sense of touch, this boy can read although he cannot see.

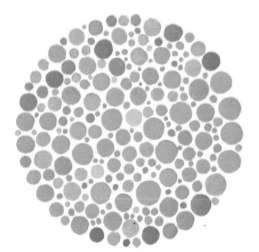

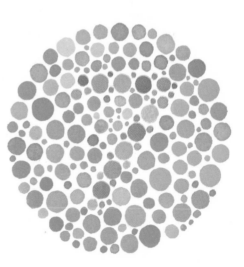

Why do some people wear glasses?

If you are born farsighted, you cannot see close objects clearly. Your lens doesn't become short and fat enough to bend the light to make a sharp image on the retina.

Wearing glasses which bend the light more will correct this condition.

If your are born nearsighted, you cannot see distant objects clearly. The lens doesn't become long and thin enough to focus the light on the retina. Again, glasses fitted after a visit to the optometrist will correct this.

As people get older, the muscles which pull the lens grow slightly weaker. Many people over 40 need glasses for reading and close work.

People often only need to wear their glasses at work or for reading.

Taking care of your eyes

A **stye** is an infection caused by germs in the tiny oil glands along the eyelid. The lump may be small but it feels very painful. Go to the doctor.

"Pinkeye" or **conjunctivitis** is an infection of the conjunctiva. It turns pink and sore — hence the name. It is also very **contagious**, or catching. If you have any eye infection, you must be careful not to use other people's towels or washcloths, and to wash your hands if you touch your eyes.

When grit gets into your eye, tears pour down to wash it out. If this doesn't work, pull your eyelid gently back and remove the grit with a clean tissue.

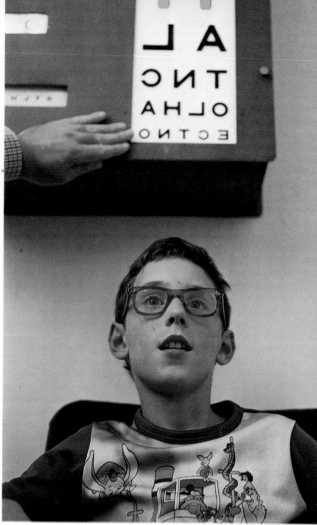

Your eyes and sight are precious and need to be looked after. Regular checkups are important. You should have foods with vitamin A in your diet to keep your eyes healthy. Milk, cheese, liver, eggs and green vegetables contain vitamin A. Make sure you always have a good light for close work. When you study, rest your eyes now and then by staring into the distance for a few seconds. Always wear protective goggles if there are splinters flying around. Never stare directly into the sun.

Regular checkups and making sure you always have a good light to work by are just two of the ways you can look after your eyesight.

15

Chapter 3

Your Sense of Touch

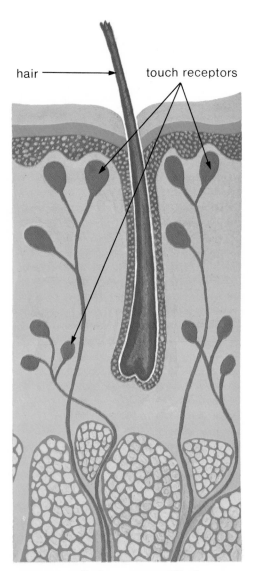

hair → touch receptors

Section of skin, magnified.

Can you imagine what it would be like to have no feeling at all? Never to feel warm and snug in bed, or refreshed after a cool swim on a hot day? Your sense of touch gives you a great deal of pleasure. Make a list of five things you enjoy feeling.

Touch receptors

These are tiny nerve endings in your skin which pick up information about touch. There are five different kinds of touch receptors: they detect light pressure, heavy pressure, pain, heat and cold. Usually more than one kind of receptor sends information to the brain.

There are touch receptors all over the surface of your skin. In some places they are crowded together, but in others they are spaced apart. Babies first learn the feel of things through their lips, which contain lots of receptors. You have to keep a careful eye on a baby — after a quick look they will put anything into their mouths, whether it's a toy or a kitchen knife!

On page 13, you saw a blind boy reading with his fingertips. You can guess from these examples that there are more touch

16

Babies "feel" things with their mouths because lips contain lots of receptors.

receptors in your lips and fingertips than anywhere else.

You can test the touch receptors very easily. Make three touch probes with corks like the ones in the diagram. Ask a friend to close his eyes and lightly press each probe in turn on his wrist. Can he tell if you are using the probe with one, two or three pins? Take turns testing other areas: the inside base of your thumb, your fingertips, upper arm, or the back of your neck.

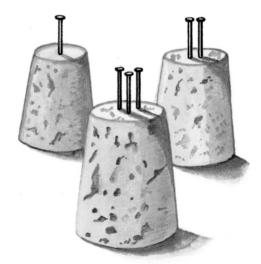

Boiling water damages your skin, and that is why it hurts. Here you can see how dangerous it is to leave pot handles within a child's reach.

Is feeling always believing?

Fill two bowls, one with warm water, the other with ice-cold. Place one hand in each bowl for a few minutes. Then put the hand from the cold basin into the warm water. Does the temperature of the warm water feel the same to both hands? If not, can you figure out why?

Why do you feel pain?

If you happen to be in pain right now, you might think it would be a good idea if there were no pain receptors! But is that really wise? Pain acts as a warning that something is going wrong. It protects you from further harm by making you stop what you are doing. It teaches you to take care of yourself because pain feels so unpleasant. What might happen to this little girl if the first burn didn't hurt?

Taking care of your skin

Apart from **hygiene**, there isn't much you can do. Except — and this is very important — you can take note of the information you receive. For example, if you feel too hot and you don't try to cool off, you may get **heatstroke**, which is very dangerous indeed.

Chapter 4
Smell and Taste

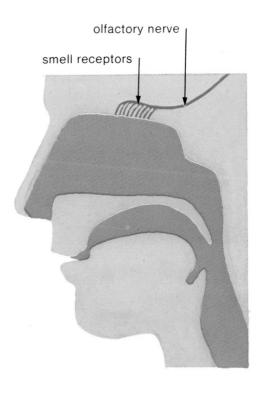

olfactory nerve

smell receptors

If you want a really good smell of something, you sniff. This pulls air up to the top of your nose. Look at the diagram and see the patch of tissue full of nerve endings. These are your smell receptors. They send information about different smells along the **olfactory nerve** to the brain. Scientists aren't sure yet how this works, but all smells are first dissolved in the watery **mucus** at the top of the nose.

There are certain smells most people like: delicious food, mown grass and clean rain. There are other smells most people find revolting, such as rotten eggs. But smells are like taste; they mean different things to different people. Some dislike the smell of tar, but others like it. Name two of your favorite smells, and two you dislike.

How smell can protect you

Smell helps you to recognize danger: fire, escaping gas, or rotting food. But you only notice a new odor for a short while — it's as if your smell receptors get used to it. This is why you can sit in a kitchen and not smell the cake starting to burn, while somebody who comes in from the outside will smell burning immediately.

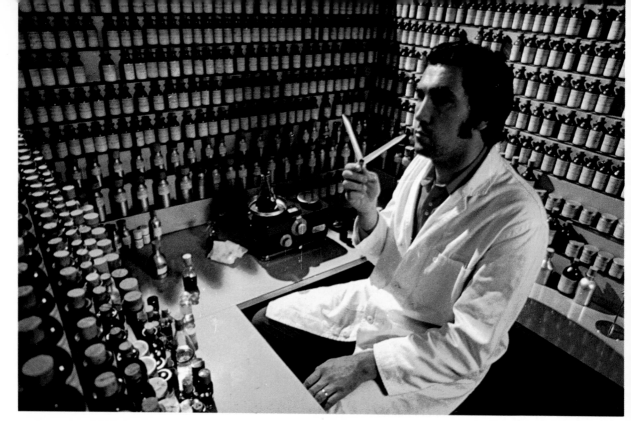

This man makes perfumes. His sense of smell is so sensitive he is called a "nose."

Some people have a much better sense of smell than others. When you have a cold you may lose your sense of smell for a while.

Your sense of taste

This seems the least important of your senses. Taste doesn't always protect you since some foods don't taste bad when they "go bad." But taste receptors do give you a lot of pleasure — imagine not being able to taste your favorite food.

Your tongue is the organ of taste. It is covered with thousands of tiny taste buds and there are also some buds on the roof of your mouth and the back of your throat. Look in the mirror with a strong magnifying glass and you can see your taste buds.

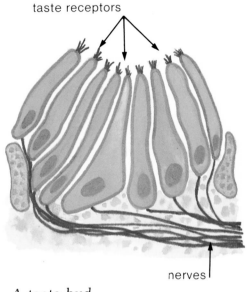

A taste bud.

Testing for taste

There are four main tastes: sweet, salt, sour and bitter. Look at the diagram and find where the taste areas are on your tongue. Most tastes are a mixture of these four. Test the different areas using sugar water, salt water, lemon juice, and strong coffee. "Clean" your tongue between each test by eating a small piece of dry bread.

Smell and taste together

On its own, your sense of taste is very weak. It's your sense of smell which adds to the taste of food. Try this out by holding your nose before and while you eat.

If you lose your sense of smell when you have a cold, you might think you have lost your sense of taste, too, but you haven't. This shows how weak your sense of taste really is.

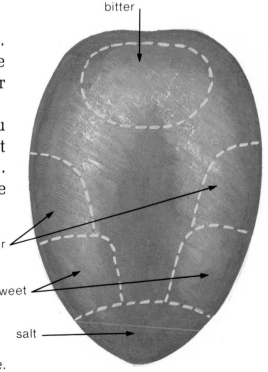

The main taste areas on your tongue.

Chapter 5

Your Ears and Hearing

Your ears gather sounds from the outside world. There are lovely sounds, such as music, and there are also warning sounds, such as traffic approaching. But the most important sound of all is that of the human voice talking. Sight or hearing — which would you miss most?

They may not have seen the bus coming, but they will hear the driver sound his horn.

The outer parts of your ear

The **pinna**, or earlobe, picks up and directs sound into your ear. You can increase the

amount of sound collected by cupping your hand behind your ear.

The canal directs sound to your **eardrum**. In the canal are tiny hairs and a waxy fluid which traps dirt and keeps the canal clean.

The inner parts of your ear

Your eardrum is a sheet of skin and muscle tightly stretched over the end of the canal. The **middle ear** behind your eardrum is filled with air, which comes up the **Eustachian tube** from your throat. The

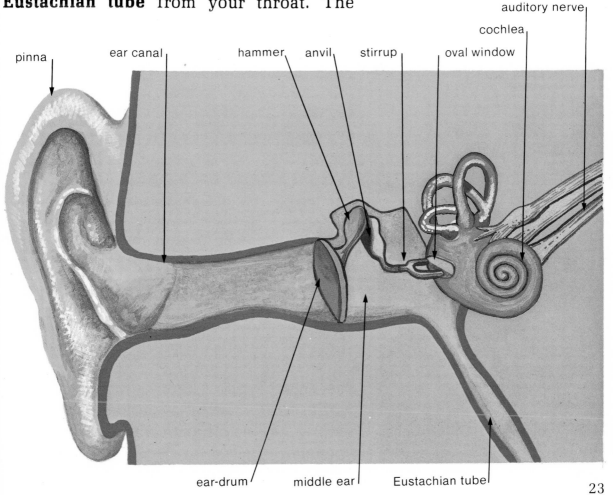

pinna   ear canal   hammer   anvil   stirrup   oval window   cochlea   auditory nerve

ear-drum   middle ear   Eustachian tube

three tiny bones, the **hammer**, **anvil** and **stirrup**, make a link across the middle ear — can you see why they have these names? The **oval window** is, in fact, another sheet of skin and is part of the **cochlea**. The cochlea looks like a snail's shell and is about the size of a pea. It is filled with fluid and nerve endings.

How do you hear sounds?

Sound travels down the canal and starts the eardrum vibrating. The three tiny bones pick up the vibrations and magnify them. The vibration passes on to the oval window, which then makes the fluid in the cochlea vibrate. The tiny nerve endings in the cochlea are your sound receptors. They pass sound information to your brain along the **auditory nerve**. Your brain interprets the information as sounds.

Why do your ears "pop"?

On the diagram of the ear, find the Eustachian tube. Now swallow hard and you will hear a "popping" sound in your head. Swallowing opens the tube, letting air in or out of your middle ear so that the air pressure is always the same on both sides of your eardrum.

When you take off or land in a plane, the air pressure outside your eardrum changes. This can feel uncomfortable and cause slight deafness. Swallow hard a few times and the feeling will wear off. You have helped the air pressure stay the same inside and outside your eardrum.

Your ears "pop" as you go up or come down in a plane.

24

Two ears are better than one

You can test this by carrying out an experiment with a friend. Your friend must be blindfolded and have one ear covered up. Now gently tap a tin can, moving farther away and backwards on your friend's "deaf" side. Note when your friend stops hearing. Is he sure where you are? If you do this again with both ears uncovered you will notice that two ears not only pick up more sound, but they also help you to judge which direction the sounds are coming from.

How we learn to speak

The most important sounds you hear are speech. At first, babies just coo and gurgle. Then they imitate the sounds made by grown-ups. All speech is learned this way, first by copying and then by practicing the sounds of words. Can you guess why it is very important for parents to talk to their babies? What would happen if a baby never heard the sound of a human voice?

Playing a game blindfolded means you have to rely on your ears instead of your eyes.

These two deaf children are learning to communicate through sign language.

Deafness

Complete or "profound" deafness is unusual. But a person who is only partly deaf finds it difficult to learn to speak. Cover your ears and imagine how shut off and lonely a deaf person might feel. Which sounds do you think you would probably miss most?

Hearing aids can magnify sounds and help some kinds of deafness. Lipreading is useful, but the deaf person must be able to see the lips of the person speaking. Sign language is a good way to communicate. Sadly, not many hearing people learn it.

It is not unusual for old people to become a little deaf. They cannot hear high-pitched sound. Keep your voice low.

Your sense of balance

Your brain needs information about your position in space — whether you are upright, leaning forward, or lying down. The sense organs which collect this information are inside your **inner ear**. They are called the **semicircular canals**.

Study the diagram and notice that each canal lies in a different position. If you could open one up, you would see it is filled with fluid and lined with tiny hairs. When you move your head, the fluid in all three canals moves as well. The tiny hairs are balance receptors, and they send information about the movements of the fluid to your brain.

Your eyes and your stretch receptors (see page 6) also help with your sense of balance. They send information to your brain at the same time as the canals. A person may be travel-sick because his brain is confused by differing information coming in. His eyes may tell him he is sitting still, but going over bumps will make the fluid in his inner ear move, and send the opposite information to the brain.

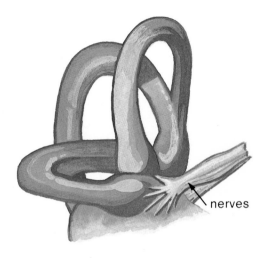

nerves

The semicircular canals.

The rides at a fairground are fun, but it is dangerous to spin around on the spot too fast. When you stop spinning, the fluid in the canals is still moving, but your brain is getting different information from your legs and eyes. This makes you feel very giddy. You may even fall down.

Why will these two chidren feel a bit giddy when the ride stops?

Taking care of your ears and hearing

The most usual kind of infection in the ear is a "middle ear infection." Germs can easily travel up the Eustachian tube to the ear—especially when you have a cold. Don't blow your nose too hard as this can force the cold germs up the tube. Go to the doctor if your ears start to hurt.

Sometimes ear wax hardens and blocks the ear canal, making you slightly deaf. But you should never try to get it out with your finger or cotton swabs. A little warm cooking oil will soften the wax and help it come out naturally.

If you live in a city, you are likely to be surrounded by noise: aircraft, cars, motorbikes and building works. Wherever you are, close your eyes and listen very carefully. How many different sounds can you hear?

Very loud noise can damage your hearing — this is noise pollution. People who work with noisy machinery should wear ear protectors for safety. Too much noise going on for too long can give you a headache. It also spoils your concentration and puts you in a bad mood.

Take care of all your senses — they are the "gateways to your brain."

The doctor is using an instrument with a light in it to check this little girl's eardrum.

Glossary

auditory nerve The bundle of nerves which carries information from the **semicircular canals** and the **cochlea** to the brain.

braille Special printing for the blind in which letters are made of raised dots. These are read by feeling them with the fingertips.

binocular vision The ability to see an object with both eyes at once. Creatures with eyes on the sides of their heads do not have binocular vision.

cochlea The spiral-shaped organ of hearing in your **inner ear**.

cones The light **receptors** in your **retina** which pick up color.

conjunctiva The thin transparent covering of the inside of your eyelids and front of your eye.

conjunctivitis An infection of the **conjunctiva**; sometimes called "pink eye."

contagious As in contagious disease; a disease which can be spread from one person to another by touching.

eardrum The sheet of skin which stretches across the end of your ear canal.

Eustachian tube The passage, about 4 cm (1½ inches) long, which connects your **middle ear** with the back of your throat.

focus To see something clearly — your **lens** brings together the rays of light falling into your eye so that they focus sharply on your **retina**.

hammer, anvil and stirrup The names of the three tiny bones in your **middle ear**.

heatstroke An illness caused by your body's overheating.

hygiene The rules of health and cleanliness.

inner ear The part of your ear which is inside your skull. It contains the **cochlea** (for hearing) and **semicircular canals** (for balance).

iris The colored part of your eye.

lens This is the round, flat transparent part of your eye behind your **pupil**. It will focus the light coming into your eye.

ligaments The bands of fiber which move the **lens** in your eye. You can read more about ligaments in another book in this series— **The Structure of Your Body.**

middle ear The air-filled section behind your **eardrum**. It contains the three tiny bones called the **hammer**, **anvil** and **stirrup**.

mucus A watery fluid produced in various parts of your body, including your nose.

olfactory This means "conected with the sense of smell," as in the olfactory nerves in your nose.

optical illusion A picture or object which misleads your brain into "seeing" something which isn't there.

optic nerve The bundle of nerves which carries information from the **rods** and **cones** of your **retina** to your brain.

oval window The sheet of skin on the surface of the **cochlea**. It carries the vibrations from your **middle ear** into your **inner ear**.

pinna The visible part of your ear; your earlobe.

pupil The round hole in the middle of your eye which lets in the light.

receptors Nerve endings in your sense organs and muscles. They collect information.

retina The thin layer of nerve cells at the back of your eye which is sensitive to light and color.

refract To bend or change the direction of a beam of light.

rods The light **receptors** in your eye which pick up dim light and enable you to see in the dark.

semicircular canals The three canals in your **inner ear**. They send information to your brain to control your sense of balance.

stimulus Something which triggers a reaction. For example, a bright light that makes the **pupil** of your eye close up.

stretch receptors Nerve endings which collect information about what is going on inside you.

stye A tiny boil in one of the oil glands at the edge of your eyelid.

Index

Picture Acknowledgements Sally and Richard Greenhill 4, 5, 6, 15, 22, 24, 25, 26, 28; Picturepoint 12, 18; Rex Features 13; Science Photo Library 8; Wayland Picture Library 14, 20, 29; Zefa 17.